ROUGH CRADLE

Also by Betsy Sholl

Late Psalm
Don't Explain
The Red Line
Rooms Overhead
Appalachian Winter
Changing Faces

ROUGH CRADLE

Betsy Sholl

Alice James Books
FARMINGTON, MAINE

10 9 8 7 6 5 4 3 2 1

Alice James Books are published by Alice James Poetry Cooperative, Inc., an affiliate of the University of Maine at Farmington.

ALICE JAMES BOOKS
238 MAIN STREET
FARMINGTON, ME 04938

www.alicejamesbooks.org

Library of Congress Cataloging-in-Publication Data
Sholl, Betsy.
Rough cradle / Betsy Sholl.
    p.   cm.
ISBN-13: 978-1-882295-73-9
ISBN-10: 1-882295-73-0
I. Title.
PS3569.H574R66 2009
811'.54—dc22   2008048460

Alice James Books gratefully acknowledges support from the University of Maine at Farmington and the National Endowment for the Arts. ❦

Cover art: Daniel Hodermarsky, "Dark Seas"
8" x 11", oil on board
Courtesy of the Daniel Hodermarsky Family Trust

For my sisters—

Jane Wood

Martha Folts

Joan Sofield, 1942–2006

CONTENTS

III

IV

ACKNOWLEDGMENTS

Heartfelt thanks to the editors of the following magazines in which these poems first appeared, sometimes in earlier versions or under different titles:

Bangor Daily News: "Love Song with Departure"; *Beloit Poetry Journal*: "Gone," "In What Furnace," "A Song in There"; *Brilliant Corners*: "Coastal Bop," "Listening to Tony Malaby at the Space Gallery," "*Acknowledgement*"; *Café Review*: "Mackerel Sky," "To the Infinitesimal"; *Chautauqua*: "Night Vision," "Hurricane Watch"; *Crab Orchard Review*: "Childhood," "The Drinking Gourd"; *Crying Sky*: "The Proposal," "*In-Flight*," "What the World Wants"; *Diner*: "*Twentieth Century Limited*"; *Field*: "Rough Cradle," "Elephant Seals"; *Green Mountains Review*: "Bird Watching," "Lullaby in Blue," "History"; *Image*: "Gravity and Grace"; *Inertia Magazine*: "Tereska"; *Off the Coast*: "The Sea Itself," "Every Note"; *Orion*: "Endless Argument"; *Poetry Miscellany*: "Mandelstam"; *Rivendell*: "Lament"; *Sou'wester Review*: "Begonia"; *Tri-Quarterly Review*: "Transport"; *West Branch*: "Elegy and Argument," "Correspondence," "The Edge of Town," "Sparrow Farming"; *Words and Images*: "Doing Time"

Thanks to the editors at *Verse Daily* for reprinting "Lament," "A Song in There," and "History." "Costal Bop" appeared in a chapbook of that title from Oyster River Press.

Special thanks to all the friends and colleagues whose eyes, ears and hearts helped these poems along: Susan Aizenberg, Lee Hope, David Jauss, Tam Neville, Clare Rossini, Natasha Saje, Leslie Ullman, and my wonderful Portland poetry group. A special thanks to April Ossmann. And always, Doug Sholl.

And it is written in the book that we shall not fear.
And it is also written, that we also shall change,
Like the words,
In future and in past,
In the plural and in isolation.
                            —Yehuda Amichai

I

THE SEA ITSELF

Here, on solid ground, a blue jay lands,
beautiful and shrill, looking right at me,
banging a seed over and over, as if

he'll never get it right—another creature
I once crudely dismissed. I'm sorry
for all my old arrogant thoughts,

for the man who followed me
one whole summer, a grabber, swallower,
a devil in Bermuda shorts. But really,

his hands were so thin and shaky,
it was easy to slip through,
all it cost me was an old blouse,

the buttons flying off into the pine needles
and white sand of our struggle.
I left him on his knees weeping,

my blue shirt dripping from his hands.
Of course, I said *No*. But I'm sorry
I said it so fiercely that day

there wasn't room for pity or anything else.
I'm not sorry I said *No* to the storm tide
that dragged me out, then tossed me back

like an undersized fish, an hysterical teenager
flung on shore. Thick quilted clouds overhead,
sand blowing through tufts of beach grass—

such a total *No,* it became a kind of *Yes,*
so the world was suddenly everything at once,
solid and shifty, stormy and calm.

For years I told this story all wrong.
Even now, my words are just a net
holding fish, while the sea itself slides through,

that slippery, unfathomable
Yes & No, that everything-at-once
impossible to name—

even if you were spared,
even if you have many more songs
than the harsh one you learned so well.

IN-FLIGHT

On Flight 293 from Atlanta,
      we passed through castling clouds
and aerial oceans, abstracted from our lives

like the contents of our bags
      the airport x-ray exposed
as gray filmy shapes, ghosts of things

we thought we couldn't do without.
      Past the slick ads, the airline magazine
showed men in battered sombreros,

woman wrapped in shawls, who spend
      their Lenten months inventing
elaborate designs out of dyed sawdust

to dribble and rake across roadside plots,
      repaving the streets for one holy week
into soul paths, swirled with their wildest prayers.

And for what, the reporter writes,
      more than once, as if perplexed
and really wanting to know: *for what*

all that money, that time spent on dust—*dust*—
      over which the Virgin
with her chipped nose and serene gaze will pass,

her makeshift palanquin teetering
      on the shoulders of young men
led by trumpeters loudly bearing down

on those fragile tableaux. At dawn it begins,
        the commotion sending birds up
out of the trees as if to proclaim

things really could change
        in a flash, in sunlight on brass.
Effort and plan, all the grand design

made just for this moment's noisy arrival—
        for the dust's bright ruin,
and for ruin to be shaken off...

DOING TIME

Prison poetry workshop

They call me "Babe" and make a kissing noise
from inside their bars and inside their rage.
Most of them are men, though they act like boys

who've played too hard and broken all their toys.
Now they're trying to break their metal cage.
They yell out "Babe," make that loud kissing noise

as if their catcalls mean they have a voice
routines and bells can't break. "It's just a phase,"
their parents must have said, when they were boys.

Don't ask what they're in for; let them enjoy
their small audience, their short time on stage:
"Hey, Babe, how about"—then that kissing noise.

In class they want to rhyme, their way to destroy
all evidence of anguish on the page.
They can't bear to remember being boys.

Some study law, some use another ploy,
daydreaming they'll do time, but never age.
"Hey, Babe" means "kiss off" to that cellblock noise,
to broken men in here since they were boys.

CHILDHOOD

In my aquarium the fish went round
and round—kissing fish and clownfish
and one very blue fish with a mouth grimmer
than Grandfather, whom we could offend
without knowing. Then no amount of running
next door to beg through the locked screen,
What did I do? would help. No amount of
saying *sorry,* stammering on the first
snakelike *S* sizzling into frayed rope.

No amount of whistling to our dog Ruff
would make him stay and not race across fields
as if running were breathing to him.
But we wanted to fondle and smooch,
to throw sticks for him to fetch right back.
We chained him up because we loved him.
Grandfather must have felt this way about
whatever was inside his head he never let out,
his long list of reasons to be bitter,

that gene he fattened and passed on
to three generations, which probably was
passed on to him, locked midway in the chain,
since his own father caught an infection
from a horse and died just days after
conceiving him. Plant matter to coal, coal
to diamond—things pressed down long enough
turn hard, then somebody finds them precious
and snarls or hisses when you get close.

I really thought if I stood outside and stared
till I saw the exact moment the streetlight
came on, my dog would speak, my fish would
let me hold his golden fin-flutter to my lips,
and my own dead father would step out from
the vanishing point at the end of our street.
It was winter, so what I got was frostbite
and a weeping mother bathing my hands
in pans of cool water. But what if

we could reel through our memories
to the exact moment before the salt
went into the wound, that moment of pure
perception before the hardening began?
Leaning from her arms to hand an apple
to a horse's brown teeth and velvet nose,
laughing at its warm breath   "Little Miracle"
my grandfather was then, child number ten,
birthed out of his mother's long black clothes.

MANDELSTAM

1891–1938

Shrunk inside an old greatcoat, stumbling,
my lips perhaps moving, I wouldn't know,
I was the murmur and seethe of terror. But there,
Voronezh, on your snow-hardened streets
where no one listened, I could whisper
to myself, wander the split paths of words
as they turned into breath's guttural ice,
and sometimes shivering, I'd sit down
half dazed on a doorstep in the dark,
as if there were no other way to be found.

Pray it is by a wife or friend
and not the hobnailed boots of police.

What happens to the swarm inside
when its honey rots? When the pilgrim's
prayers have hardened, so what buzzed
at his lips is trapped in amber? Any way
it's told, history's a bad translation.
Where I went, the road ends in a heap
of confiscated past, a dump
where dogs and the poor and the ghost
of a poet rummage, until the wind
grows weary of swirling, and lets us drop.

CALIFORNIA MORNING

February, Avila Beach

To winter-dull ears what a reveille,
this medley of finches, and who knows
what—west coast jays, titmice, chickadees,
mockers? It's the gladdest ruckus
we've heard in months, little bird brawls,
brushing twigs so they tip last night's rain,
splattering us with drips and chirps.

We lean out over the rail, aching
our necks to look up the skirts of trees,
wanting to *get-it-get-it,* go from tease
to that sweet spot the binoculars
could zoom us into, zip us up among
those yellow and blue flirts we half wish
we could be, flitting in and out

of the limbs, flaring our wings, singing
got-it-got-it, tail feathers fanned—and if
not that, can we at least drink our tea
and be at peace in the *almost,* in the *brief,*
even in the *not,* the flyby *without,*
in the tight space between stem
and leaf, between *longing* and *let-go?*

IN WHAT FURNACE

The long neck, the windblown waterfall of tail—
what vision flickers in my daughter's eyes
as she stands on a fence rail, saying there's fire
in the mare's mane backlit by late sun?
Fire, too, I think, in her own bright hair.

In what furnace, wrote mad William Blake,
asking what force makes tiger and lamb,
what eye finds the lost boy dressed in soot,
finds inside the destitute old man,
the weeping child—mad burning William Blake

who looked and saw the world inside out,
flame at its core, smoldering, God-made.
Flame still, we see, in the dark chestnut
of this horse's eye, in the mystery
of her tongue, tooth, lip, each flick of ear

and running stream of whinnies, in her coat
growing winter-long and shaggy: What hand,
what faceless breath flares these nostrils,
tosses the head, blows the straw of this tail
over the coals rippling inside her flanks?

Out of what furnace was she drawn and bred
into racer, warrior, hauler, vehicle,
into that creature little girls love and men stake
their fortunes on? What flame in my daughter
makes her jiggle her apple and call?

From my womb this child, leaning toward
huge breath, toward blaze. And me at the kiln door,
holding her back, recalling my own first horse—
gone now, as so much is gone, as coal sheen
goes to ash flake, to clinker of black lace,

gone, but still glowing in night-sweat dreams—
his burnished flanks and jittery side steps,
that excellent memory intent on
frightening me again, just where he first
backed me against the stall, over and over

raising his head, glaring wildly, stomping
his foot so close to mine, he could have crushed it
if he wanted, but chose instead to impress
on me the hot twist of sinew, the hammer
of his strength, the lit forge of his eye.

HURRICANE WATCH

My death is made of water, thick with sand,
that storm-gray grit, stirred up sea bottom
   where bodies drift with their blank stares,
crushed by waves like trucks bearing down
   full speed. If you survive that rip and suck,
and rise back up? You'll feel with each gust
   of wind a wave starting to curl, its glitter
of sand an itch in your scalp, a sting of salt
   in your throat. What is sleep then, but panic
relaxed into a black chute as you stop flailing
   and let yourself slide? The scariest part,
that gap between blackout and beach,
   not knowing how you arrived—or *if,*
you sometimes think—whether mercy
   saved you, or chance just slowed your fate.
Some have stories: ministers of rescue
   or answered prayers for a wave's whale surge
to disgorge them on shore. Along the beach,
   at clam shacks and bars they tell their tales:
who took their hand, what lifeboat appeared.
   To them the future is sure. But if you
wake up limp and coughing on an empty shore,
   no one in sight, all your life you wonder.
What can you say about the future
   when you can't grasp the past? Every drink
reminds you of what almost drank you.
   Do some people look at the sea and not see
death coming in waves, in swells and heaves,
   falling cabinets of green glass? Beautiful, yes.
But once you've gone under, tumbled
   through eddies of watery shards,

worlds wild with gravity's lash and plunge,
  if you can't say for sure how or why,
just *that* you woke on shore, flimsy
  but still alive, then what's the difference?
Swirl of sand grains or stars—
  when your head hits bottom, they're the same
bright stirred-up cloud of pure unknowing.

LOVE SONG WITH DEPARTURE

The ocean dips and surges in the heat,
heaves its breast, I almost said,
like any earnest suppliant at the altar of longing.

The bemused mystic who is half my mind—
well, maybe an eighth—asks why it isn't enough
just to breathe, to sit among beach roses

beside the changing tide. If it's all light
in the end, why not practice now, bleaching
out the shadows of the mind? Even stones

become light, you said last night, your love voice
heating up, free-falling through the atmospheres
of our desire. What I understood

was your breath falling warm on my ear,
melting my clamorous thoughts.
Did I say anything back? This morning,

watching your tail pipe's cloud dissolve
in the air, I wanted to eat stones, dress myself
in a shark's slinky scales that will slice

anyone who runs his hands along my thigh
the wrong way, which is any way that isn't yours.
Tomorrow, I'll feel the same.

II

ELEPHANT SEALS

Muffled thunder like clouds rolling over
in sleep, and mirrored underneath—
such gray sodden bodies, enormous slugs

with Spandexed buttocks and thighs.
One, with his long dangling nose
like something lunar, tumorous, lumbers

across the sand, nudging through others who arf,
who rise on fins, then belly-flop down.
Easy to argue from nature anything

at all—dead end in evolution's maze,
or evidence of God's wild earthy wit.
But the bulls argue over their harems,

one youth galumphing toward a battle-scarred
alpha who rears and roars, till the upstart
backs off, biding his time. Around them

the sea sputters, rain pocks the sand, the pod
piles up. If this is the utterly other,
still, when one drowsy-eyed mother,

lolling as her baby nuzzles in to nurse,
lifts a fringed, finger-like fin to scratch,
everyone watching feels an itch.

LULLABY IN BLUE

The child takes her first journey
through the inner blue world of her mother's body,
blue veins, blue eyes, frail petal lids.

Beyond that unborn brackish world so deep
it will be felt forever as longing, a dream
of blue notes plucked from memory's guitar,

the wind blows indigo shadows under streetlights,
clouds crowd the moon and bear down on the limbs
of a blue spruce. The child's head appears—

midnight pond, weedy and glistening—
draws back, reluctant to leave her first home.
Blue catch in the mother's throat,

ferocious bruise of a growl, and out slides
the iridescent body—fish-slippery
in her father's hands, plucked from water

into such thin densities of air,
her arms and tiny hands stutter and flail,
till he places her on her mother's body,

then cuts the smoky cord, releasing her
into this world, its cold harbor below
where a blue caul of shrink-wrap covers

each boat gestating on the winter shore.
Child, the world comes in twos, above and below,
visible and unseen. Inside your mother's croon

there's the hum of an old man tapping his foot
on a porch floor, his instrument made from one
string nailed to a wall, as if anything

can be turned into song, always what is
and what is longed for. Against the window
the electric blue of cop lights signals

somebody's bad news, and a lone man walks
through the street, his guitar sealed in dark plush.
Child, from this world now you will draw your breath

and let out your moth flutter of blue sighs.
Now your mother will listen for each one,
alert enough to hear snow starting to flake

from the sky, bay water beginning to freeze.
Sleep now, little shadow, as your first world
still flickers across your face, that other side

where all was given and nothing desired.
Soon enough you'll want milk, want faces, hands,
heartbeats and voices singing in your ear.

Soon the world will amaze you, and you
will give back its bird-warble, its dove call,
singing that blue note which deepens the song,

that longing for what no one can recall,
your small night cry roused from the wholeness
you carry into this broken world.

GONE

Far back in the hills behind the pastures past the stand
   of oaks where cows graze undergrowth down
to bare ground   through denser woods
     brambled ravines   not a cloud in the sky
not a nest in the ground   till suddenly a grouse
     startles straight up   scraping my cheek   a stun

     so my own heart half copters out   almost without a self
     then   legs briared   sensing wolves or worse
I walk on   fearing the woods won't like me

     come to an overgrown field   sunlight glinting on
what   radiators old sinks doors worn down to unhinged
     oblivion   rust eating through rust   not one
undented pot with lid   not a toaster with wire attached
     just pieces of bridge   blue broken gazebo
     tiny and chipped   willow ware hard-caked in dirt

     Aphid earthworm shy beetle scuttling off
good daughters of earth   cleaning house   filling
     the land   with what it would rather forget

is there a somewhere   for everything   and if not
     the dark side of the moon   then this hidden ravine
stumbled on by fear   inner tube heating coil clock face
     staring up   Good daughters   you spiders and slugs
how I feared you appearing   in ones and twos
     on my doorstep   I knew your land by sight

driving past   not by downed limb rabbit hole thicket
     not by ditch   where what once worked   is inert
     swaddled in dirt   earth pierced by bed spring jay shriek

Earnest daughters   endlessly swarming gnawing
cracked lampshade pitted soup ladle   all that was human
      gone feral   the dizzy acceleration
looking down that deep well   teetering   the terror
      and thrill of it   Spider beetle worm rot mold
you endless invincible doers   and undoers

      on my doorstep   in the woods   emptying one space
filling another   spinning weaving   Oh daughters
      all things made   unmade

LAMENT

Clinch Haven Farm, Big Stone Gap, Virginia

Fog dense as a bed sheet draped at the window,
and through that white blindness come
the eerie cries of cows moaning in the field
like a whole mothering universe calling

for lost sons—trucked off to auction in the night.
On grief's scale these wails fall lower than
the shriek that stunned us when we strolled past
the funeral home just as its doors opened,

and a gaunt woman went slack, sinking
to the floor, sobbing for a son killed,
O Lord, no. The funeral men tried to lift her,
but her legs refused to bear that grief's weight.

Why should sorrow rise? Why should it proceed
in orderly fashion out to the waiting
black car? In autumn the sun doesn't rise
above the mountain till nine, the fog

doesn't so much lift as narrow to one long
trail of exhaust, as if the world had layers
and scrims. Steam swirls over hay bales
as the cows feed, suddenly tired, stretching

their necks for one last sob, milk sacks heavy.
But in fog everything dissolves—goldenrod,
corn stubble, guardrails. Blankness so thick
it seems a hand stretched out might never come back.

If grief has a totem, if there are guides
through the lead-weighted air, it must be
these cows bunched at the fence, pressing so close
they'll leave tufts of hair in the barbs. Lulled now,

they wait, barely visible, their solid bodies
on stilt-thin legs, enormous eyes watching
over a world thick with veils the light won't pierce—
Lord, not for hours. Not for a long time.

A SONG IN THERE

To stave off trouble, the old bluesmen are singing,
without a doubt, singing—on doorsteps, in bare yards
with folding chairs tipsy on tree roots. No tape rolling,
no old rattling film, no spotlight, gold tooth, big car.

Forgive me, my heroes, for thinking this tragic,
that a front porch with crickets and night fog
isn't enough, a dusty juke joint with straw-strewn floor
buoyant under sore but dancing feet.

I want to believe that even books burned to ash
were worth the long nights of their making, that a song
drifting on invisible waves still exists somewhere
however faint, washing an unknown shore.

You who were not recorded to be touched up
and played back later, did you love the raw world more,
love the shy songbird's refusal to be seen?
My mentors, you who heard a minor chord,

a blue note struck two fields away, and ambled over
to swell the sound, joining the blue breakup, breakdown,
the song talking back to the battered life—forgive me
for even once wanting to sit in the sleek car

airbrushing through town. In its wake the world
resumes, briar and dust, heartbeat and sky, nest
squalling with hunger. And there, broke or flush,
blind or sighted, you sang. Traveling by hay wagon,

boxcar, jalopy, fingers like knotted sticks, a thicket
in your voice, on unpaved corners for spare change,
you sang. Over you the clouds would bundle and shred,
the night send out sparks. Then earth closed over.

Now the air's full of echo and remix.
Still, in my mind's graveyard, I am laying flowers
at your unmarked feet, fingering the Braille
of a tree's lichened trunk, all splotch and ridge—

your monument, bearing wounds where limbs were
cut off. I know the music's in there, somewhere
rising, leaf thirst and bent note, a song in there,
root-crooned, wind-strummed and rising.

GRAVITY AND GRACE

*Grace fills empty spaces, but it can only enter
where there is a void to receive it.*
—Simone Weil

Simone Weil, it's hard to concentrate on you
with those three boys on the next bench
blowing up balloons and letting them go,
all squirt and grunt, fizzling into—

the void, you'd probably say. And leaving
a void too—if spent breath becomes exhaust,
if everything we do ends up empty.
So, prayer becomes a little death

as we pour our desires into words
that fill to bursting, then leave our lips
to corkscrew and sputter, spitting out air,
selfless, anonymous enough to rise.

Now the boys race up the slide, all high-fives
and laughter, blowing off gravity, while I read
you'd like to be blown away, see a landscape
as it is when I am not there—as if the self

blocks God the way bodies block light.
Thus your executor was to destroy
all record of your mind—those notebooks filled
with stark meditations as Hitler railed,

as death camps filled and ghettos burned. *Love is
not consolation,* you wrote, *it is light,*
meaning that fierce headlamp of attention
which leaves the self in shadow and trains

its high beam on the void where prisoners
huddle under gravity's dark weight—
and grace, if it comes, comes in secret,
to those struck dumb, trembling in the glare.

THE DRINKING GOURD

For homework we were to connect the stars
into constellations along dotted lines,
but when I stepped outside, those lines tore
apart like perforations, and the stars
scattered. Chicken feed tossed in a dark yard,
water flung from a bucket.

Underneath that crazy fizz of light
I was illiterate, able to read
just one shape, the dipper, what fugitive
slaves called "the drinking gourd" in the song
our teacher sang about the North Star
leading them through dense woods and bogs.

When the evening news showed mothers
shrieking at little kids trying to walk
to school, or big kids getting yanked
off their soda fountain stools,
I'd step outside. No color on our old
black-and-white, just grownups snarling.

Away from the slant of window light,
under the sky's bright litter, I'd look
for that drinking gourd, and shiver.
Twig snap, dried vines, night things
grabbing from behind. Then something new—
those raging faces, ready to tear apart

the children walking slowly, their eyes fixed
on the door straight ahead, while around them,
barely held by sawhorses and police,
mothers gone feral bared their teeth
and screamed as if the stars
were shooting from the sky.

THE EDGE OF TOWN

I loaded stones from the Irish coast into my suitcase,
   till I felt like that overwrought saint who,
      instead of picking one ribbon as offered,
         grabbed the entire box and ran. I would have
      taken the whole wild western coast, wave-strewn
layers of sediment pressed down and heaved up,

left as rubble, then smoothed by the sea's
   agitated prancing in its rocky stall.
      It was that rough shore I wanted. And more,
         its long view back to something older than age.
      Those two huge upright stones with a stone slab
capping them left to mark the dead

as if death were an old implacable god,
   an ancient relentless one to stand before
      dumbstruck. Centuries of cattle had rubbed
         the rock black. Five thousand years of rain
      had pocked the roof. Cloud shadows blew
across the flimsy moments we stood there

at that narrow gateway back, past the past
   into grunt and squat, lightning strike,
      peat smolder, into a time when time was hunger
         and weather, when heaving one heavy thing
      on top of another was the loudest prayer,
though whatever they said is pressed now

into a thin ribbon of quartz. In the distance,
   gulls turned, first into small glints, then into
      nothing at all. That must be how, if the past
         had eyes, it would see us, dizzy with
         disappearing, cheeks pressed against rock,
      a blustery wind scrubbing our faces,

in one afternoon worn down to foam scud,
   mica flash, bone—one afternoon and a storm
      out at sea, on whose edges we walked
         picking up stones. And here they are,
         heaped at the foot of our stairs, prayers
      from before beads, before chisels cut dates

into rock to stop the dissolve. Gems
   too wild for a jeweler to tame, too rough
      for anyone's finger or neck. Faceless clocks
         calibrated to measure eons, not hours. We wanted
         to remember what had already forgotten us,
      since when we stopped at the edge of town

to look back, the sea had turned away,
   that light-seared, cloud-blown battering sea,
      just a glint now through the window
         of an old stone church, wild in its ruin,
         waiting for wind and water to batter it more,
      and unmortar, possess it completely.

TRANSPORT

On the radio: illegal roads gouged through the rain forest.
Then I'm out of range and the station's gone to screech—

or else the crew's pressed deeper in to lush green static,
to eerie tropical birds, shrieks more like the damned

enduring Dante's bad weather, his mist and barren trees
ten times worse than this mid-coast November.

Be Prepared to Stop a sign reads, as if up ahead's
a broken bridge or rubble-blocked road.

In Florence Dante was superintendent of roads,
till factions and papal graft forced him out,

never to return by any highway or street,
though he'd wander plenty.

Sitting in line behind the flag woman,
I smell asphalt and think somebody's getting it,

someone's cursing or pleading, up to his neck in tar
as the steam roller bears down, its driver working the gears

like a tiny brain moving some huge lumbering world.
Dumb fate—or do we get what we deserve?

Trapped in the noise of giant graders, I picture
brightly plumed birds dust-drenched in roadside scrub,

grit in their throats, a song lost for each half-mile
of progress, something broken for each thing made.

Power paves over, conspiracy rewrites the signs.
So much for my childhood odes to quahog chips,

starfish, swirls of moon snail mixed in with the macadam
of my road—mere filler I see now,

though when rain pulled the clouds away, blue sky
gleamed at our feet—little stone novas, shards of sunset.

Could it be true, all the way to heaven *is* heaven,
as St. Catherine said? It would take a saint to see that

through switchbacks and sheer drops, those hard roads
leading the exile to yet another town, another sleepless bed.

Dante conjured a paradise out of pure swoon, the dream
of one whose weary eyes have replayed miles

of rubble and ditch and dusty light, through which he sees
the road in airy shimmers begin to rise.

BIRD WATCHING

Maybe it's not a lie to say my mother
was once a bird, or two really: one who'd
soar, blue into blue, the other a groundling
endlessly pecking. How she loved binoculars,
loved to reverse *distant* and *close*,

to be off grieving on a high branch
while I tugged at her skirt. What she had to say
about joy could fill an ashtray left out
in the wind, so perhaps it's from her I learned
to tremble on hearing the word *future*,

to worry that the universe can't just expand
forever, and to cringe when the Chinese fortune
says my luck will change. I have to ask
what it is now. Then watching neon rain
splash the restaurant window, those hot pink

mysterious characters flashing off and on,
I wonder if it's all one great unfolding,
impossible to name, so a bird
flying off doesn't have to mean *gone*,
it could mean: look at that bright going.

III

CORRESPONDENCE

Another rain cloud arrives by mail:
glum words, the paper thick and damp,

a limp handshake that won't shake off.
Even Christ stands at the door and knocks.

But these letters slip through the mail slot,
already in the house when I get home,

a new one every day, its voice crowding my mind,
so like me at my saddest, I can't tell us apart—

that sigh released when the envelope's torn,
the little news of laundry and books, a cold,

a cooking class, a neighbor's hurtful words.
Wet handkerchiefs made of paper, thin pages

recycled from other letters
that have had their say, been sent back to pulp,

and pressed blank for someone else's need.
The letters pile up, days and weeks of them, too many.

They slip off the table onto the floor, canceled
by a boot tread, and the sight terrifies—

to think of a knock and the door latched tight,
so many smudged lives left unread,

their inky serifs never sparked and reborn
in another's mind. Even monks alone in damp cells,

concocting ink out of dried insect larvae,
out of rainwater mixed with wine and sulfuric acid

poured over nails, wrote their pleasures
and pains in the margins of the text,

as if the anonymous, too, need a witness,
and holy writ knew to make space

for its scribes' stiff hands and agues,
for a cat's cryptic distraction.

Now, we have e-mail and answering machines.
I called my teacher's apartment for days

after she died, to keep her voice
from erasing itself in my mind. But I was afraid

to leave a message, afraid nothing
would stop its fray and drift through earless air.

O letters awkwardly skittering across my floor
like drunks thrown out of bars, wounded angels,

one wing torn off or never formed—
your small voice makes me bend close,

till I can't help but hear how loneliness
calls to its own.

TWENTIETH CENTURY LIMITED

I used to think a train whistle fathered me,
story my mother once told, then refused

to repeat, as if conception's not a subject
for the conceived. It hardly had to do with me:

four A.M. milk train, my father's wakened passion,
my mother having watched his kindness

to strangers the night before, wanting
that warmth inside her . . .

So, in the pre-dawn I became a passenger
riding their wail, offspring of love cries

too quickly morphed into the *all aboard*
carrying my father's coffin back East,

the long sigh of my mother's widowhood.
Even now, the late-night rumble makes me shudder

as those wheels clatter through town,
arrivals and departures riding the same track.

HISTORY

In Mongolian bars now Genghis Khan beer's
the rage, and in markets Genghis Khan soap,

pillowcases, gasoline conquer new worlds—
centuries after those horsemen first rode out

behind their commander's trumpets and flags,
eyeing dust devils up ahead. Their mission:

to level towns. Or so we've been told.
But history's written by those who can write,

by townsfolk left behind, who put down in ink
what first occurred in a blur of dust and blood.

Those riders didn't take long to saddle up
and move on. What good were towns to them,

their eyes full of sand's blinding drifts dervishing
on wind shears? What was history to those

who felt sand at their heels, erasing their tracks
as they rode in the name of the great Khan:

Genghis, meaning something like *Ocean*
for its breadth and depth, for those waves

of warriors racing on as wind whipped
their backs, on and on toward land's end,

toward water as far as they could see—
endless, blue, undrinkable water.

TERESKA

After the photo by David Seymour, "Tereska,
A Child in a Residence for Disturbed Children,"
Poland, 1948

She's been given chalk and asked to draw
a picture of home, so it's hard to see
in her spiraled lines an abstract design,
hard to think "antic delight in pure form,"
when she stands beside the board, looking
fixed and wary, having just mapped a world
slashed with barbed wire, a world crossed out,
going up in chalky flames, yellow smoke
scribbling its dust over roofs, curtains,
books and dolls, whatever a house once held.
Someone's put a ribbon in her hair,
but she's hardly a little girl, glaring
as if to warn: ask for something pretty,
and she'll cat-scratch with that chalk,
claw and hiss—this *is* her home now,
this world found only by tearing up the map,
this town without streets, house with no mother,
no music, no lights, just a heap of rubble
where a mind lives hunched down and feral,
defending the one thing it knows.

ROUGH CRADLE

I

We'd yank at the pull rope, watching rainbows ooze,
till the drizzle and sputter took hold. *No Wake*
the sign read, so we'd ease through the sleepy channel.
But when the river opened, we revved that old Evinrude

and aimed straight for the biggest swells,
till salt spray, engine noise, wave slap drove out all talk.
School talk, shop talk, radio and God talk, our mother—
measure up their favorite phrase.

The shore was a green shaggy blur soaking up noise.
Light on the water scoured our eyes. When we hit the inlet
we'd idle back so fast our own wake almost swamped us,
sinking us down into water's rough cradle.

                                    We didn't talk.
It was that rocking we wanted, waves slapping the hull,
all meaning sea-blasted out.

II

Once I watched the talk drain from a bed of lilies.
From the courthouse steps, after weeks of jury duty,

weeks of accusations, defenses, pleas, all meaning
was fly drone, a measureless swarm. I heard alibis,

angles, odds, all the old frauds, turn into syrupy sludge,
clogged-up engine voice with its futile cough and sob.

44

Later, in the grocery, I watched a woman roll her eyes
and cluck over tabloid headlines, then tell her friend

she couldn't imagine abusing a child. If I had words then,
I would have said, *You didn't try very hard.*

I would have followed her to her flag-decked car,
instead of going home to sit in my kitchen

in the same nightgown for days, staring at the same book
open to the same incomprehensible page:

III

Jonah lulled by the lilt and list rocking his hammock
          in the hold.
Jonah when the waves rose, when the pitch and roll worsened.
Asleep in the closet when the cargo's cast out, Jonah,
          back turned to God, the eye of the storm.
Jonah in the ship spinning over its own sinking,
crying *Toss me out*, plummeting down, seaweed at his throat.
Jonah in the belly, the baleen, ambergris, bone and gore.

In Nineveh he cried the length of the town, his voice a wild
          breach and fluke slap of God.
Housewives, merchants, judges, crooks, the broken, the bitter
          dropped to their knees, splashing ashes over their heads.
They didn't talk, they wailed.
And the invisible calamitous wave swelling above them
withdrew, just as it had curled, ready to crash.
Measuring up? Hadn't they measured *down*, their reach
          into the wrack of their own drowning?

I called my sister then, not to talk, but to bring back
the sound, when the engine's cut, and the water's
          soft lapping is sweet all over.

45

NIGHT VISION

I thought city hall might be blown up, but not my street.
The bombs are smart, they can tell what's residential,
can find a building at night after its workers have gone,
just papers left to fly out of steel cages, wheeling like gulls,
only silent, no rusty hinge, no old fan belt of a cry.

I thought the courthouse's wood panels might be curled
by the heat, names of accused and accuser mingled in ash.
Maybe the police station, chunks of concrete collapsing
on the garage full of confiscated cars, thin plumes
of smoke rising through skeletal beams.

But not my street with its flower baskets,
its seven schools, two pizza shops, its butcher
selling gourmet food, its shoe repairs, its sewing shop
run by two Koreans. I didn't expect to see
lawns seared, porches charred, windows blown out,

our family portraits scattered on the street in pools
of water from the firefighters' anxious dousing.
I didn't expect people wailing, shaking their fists,
bent over limp children who'd been walking to school.
But I was wrong, wrong. None of this happened,

not here on this street, not downtown. None of it
occurred anywhere outside the green night lens
of my own troubled sleep's lit-up synapses,
my foolish dream which couldn't tell fear from truth,
could not distinguish between *here, there, us* and *them.*

THE PROPOSAL

Marry me is what the wind said, I think,
in a real voice. Though it might have been
something else, wind only the messenger,
invisible page. Still, I turned to see
what was there, even far off,

even light-years away, and heard it
again, from a cricket this time,
the tiny *me, me,* growing louder
like something big wanting to rush in.
So I whirled around, and a young spruce

said something like *marry,* I swear,
and the gray smoke of a squirrel's tail
whispered it too, while the moon lingered
in a pale negligee, singing, *I do, I do.*
Is the whole world a wedding—

even as it is, heaped ash trays
dumped in the street, palsied children
lined up for the bus, flapping, drooling
wet cookie crumbs down their coats?
A car blasted its bass. A crow screeched.

A sudden shadow seemed to warn: Every
minute held back is a snuffed wick.
Trying to slow this down, I lifted the brick
from the newsstand just as a gust came up
and whisked the paper out of my hands,

pages of brides grinning in newsprint gowns,
as if singing to all the world: Spatter us
with road grit, kiss us with spittle and crumbs,
tumble us against the schoolyard fence,
oh dearly beloved, dearly whoever you are.

SPARROW FARMING

The room was dark and crammed with writers
in the photo labeled *Gotham Book Mart, 1948,*
and its caption in the magazine asked,
"Can you name all the literary lights?"

Already I wanted to leave, drift down the page
to the white space at the bottom, a boxed ad
with just the words *Sparrow Farming*
and a phone number, its digits

like little birds pecking at a hedgerow,
or flocking to a wire above a snowy field.
The bookshop could have been a cage,
with sparrows perched at different heights: Bishop

leaning against a shelf, a pale Miss Moore seated,
Jarrell on a low stool, while Auden looks down
from a ladder, remarkably unwrinkled.
They were all I knew among a dozen others,

numbered left to right, and I didn't like it
when the editor asked, upside down,
at the bottom of the next page: "Well—
how did you do?" And then, as if to tease:

"If you didn't get at least fifty percent, you—"
but the rest of the sentence wasn't there, or anywhere.
So, *you* have to fill in your own consequence:
"you don't belong," "don't have a clue…"

But what on earth is sparrow farming—
breeding those scrappy little birds who sing
from dawn to dusk, hungry to full and back?
Looking again, I see I've misread: *Sparrow Framing*—

as in containing some flitting moment,
that human need to count and be counted,
to make a camera flash, even if it only
catches the short stasis before someone

gets up to leave and another takes his place—
someone who will step outside the shop
into a gust of rain or snow pushing him
a little faster than he meant to go.

LISTENING TO TONY MALABY
AT THE SPACE GALLERY

Portland, Maine

Heavy meds have muted my friend, but still
he's into this set, ending with just breath

brushing along the sax's brass hall. He's cool
with the room's bare pipes and exposed beams,

talking sunsets he's seen from fishing boats
far out at sea: *colors like the insides*

of every kind of fruit, the insides of space.
He closes his eyes and leans in as the trio resumes,

not asking what to make of the stunning jumble,
not straining after pattern or tune—that's me,

till finally something breaks. Gut rumble
of sax, drum torrent, or the pianist's forearm

thundering down on the Wurlitzer—
why try to figure it out? Would a sunset ask?

Does the sea need to name its waves?
White water and sonic surge, wild eddies and swells,

we go under and come back up
past thought, no need to separate wave

from water or air—not that we're prepared
to dissolve in either. But afterwards, outside,

when my friend grins like he's been somewhere
totally unexpected, some far world's end,

I grin back. Then he wheels his arms,
as if to catch the music and help it on

through the night's cold breath
into a kind of silence that still resounds,

the way after leaving a museum, art
is everywhere, outline of roofscapes, light

in a dozen shades, stark shadows
on lamp-lit cindery streets, lone figure

in the distance, turning once to wave—my friend
growing bigger out there, where I can't see.

ACKNOWLEDGEMENT

On your street, sidewalk bricks up-tumbled
    by glacial roots, I walked looking down,
        not up, went slowly, though I wanted
to rush—then was stopped by a copper beech,
    low-spread branches, all wrinkle and stretch,
        trunk like gray animal hide.
Blue sky and such a longing to slip inside, swoon
    through limbs into wine-dark leaves.
        As if desire's meant to go
unfilled, longing the one sure thing wired in...
    flowers in every bed: hollyhock,
        hibiscus, begonia,
cosmos—different names for you.
    Birds flitting into leaves, flirting,
        backlit, hiding, their songs
inconsolably sweet. Silver flash,
    train tracks. Fray of one
        dissolving cloud. In my ears,
breath bruised through saxophone tube
    and bell, coming out brazen
        as birds with red antennae,
bright-feathered crowns I saw once
    in aviary heat and steam, and wondered,
        was that your thought:
make some like this, others naked so they'll long
    themselves into feathers and song?
        Red-tipped yellow drinking song,
iridescent-eyed metallic screech, shades of brown
    haunting-and-not-seen eerie call leading
        deeper into bewilderment's forest,

where some reach for what will undo them,
        some take the not-having, that hunger inside
                everything swirls around,
and make something of it. Breath blown
        through empty brass growing bigger
                as it's given out. As if Your ideas
could ever be known: You, whose copper beech
        boggles the mind, half-invisible,
                erupting with song.

IV

MACKEREL SKY

I thought it would be a good thing to look
at the sky ten minutes a day. But after just one

I'm dizzy, tipping my lawn chair and falling
the way on the edge of sleep you plummet

without ever leaving your bed. Autumn
west wind blowing big cumulus puffs,

heaping them up on the eastern edge
as if whole heavens could topple and plunge.

How good my little scrap of dried lawn
suddenly feels, its last yellow flowers,

last color to leave the blind—and I'd like
to be a little blind myself to this surge

of migration overhead, thick exhaust
of paradise revving its engines

to leave us behind. Rorschach sky, mackerel,
buttermilk—and remember the mushroom skies

we watched every year in school, that urgent
over-voice promising the great black swells

would make us safe, as we crouched
under the gum-spackled wooden sky of our desks.

Puzzle it out: *our* planes, *our* bombs,
our school, no other enemy in sight...

When annihilation drill was over,
we'd go back to numbers or art, drawing

houses that might any minute implode,
picket fences ready to tumble up.

BEGONIA

Each evening I believe in the everlasting, and fear
by dawn blight will have crept into the garden.

But each morning there you are, watery blossoms
dripping from the lip of multiple green faucets,

a magician's trick of scarf after soft yellow
and orange scarf rippling from a sleeve.

How to name your layers of petalwork,
your shades of peach, apricot, lemon, goldfinch—

labia it's all right to look at? Again
and again your bright orange pods burst

into a bush full of canaries, each one singing.
Still, I can't forget that tyrants tend gardens,

Stalin ordered executions among bright buds
which continued to unfurl. Such fragrant treachery.

Or were they earth's efforts to dissuade?
Clearly, you have no ill will,

so if there's a judgment, and a witness is needed
to testify against us, let it be you,

before whom the only penance is awe.
O delicate teacups with so many rims

drinking's unthinkable—
O galaxy of florescent stars fluttering down

on the just and the unjust, long into September.

WHAT THE WORLD WANTS

On this northern rim of the world,
the cold seeps through worn collars
like the ocean's iciest breath, like death,

or the whole second shift, spilling out
of the plant into night's deep freeze,
unscarfed throats bait for the wind's teeth.

At week's end I take my thin paycheck
into an overpriced shop and linger
under the saleswoman's chilly glare,

fingering soft weaves I can't afford,
dangling fringe in my palm, weighing rent
against cashmere, cable against chenille.

In the three-way mirror I line up to eye
my triplicate selves: one face oozes
with desire, one scowls, furrowed up,

feeling duped by vanity's profiteers,
the middle one sighs and turns away,
baring her chapped throat to the world.

But inside my patched jacket and scuffed boots,
that self stands on the twilit street
and can't help seeing the sky turn pale silk,

its mist like rain tamed and spun into fringe.
She'll stomp to shake it off, mutter about deceit's
flimsy gauze draped over necessity.

And yet, under the sky's late glow, its dark
translucent blue nothing can duplicate,
she has to think maybe the world wants

a little shimmer and gloss, wants its workers
when the bottle's empty, the table bare,
to notice the cloth's lavish folds.

NOCHE OSCURA

Oh guiding night
Night sweeter than dawn.
—St. John of the Cross

This morning I walked too quickly through
the green depth of fir trees, so the birds
were just a brief mood, small buzz of thought.
But if the titmice were saying *me me me me*
like rude kids mimicking opera singers,
still in the fir-fringed cold, they were birds,

frankly birds, whose calls pierce the air
and dissolve—birds saying whatever they say:
cat below, chickadee, food, food,
and something else which, even if I sat
in those boughs all night, I wouldn't know.
Night—I look up, and there it is,

huge eye at the window filling the glass.
I see in its gleaming pupil a smear
of tilted bookshelves, paintings loosened
into blotches of color, the ceiling dropped low
with black branches stretched across it,
and in that dark reflection, I am a smudge

halfway to oblivion and clutching a phone
as if talk could hold it back, as if I could
ring the hospital and keep her
from drifting away—as if I hadn't just seen
through night's thick lens how a figure can blur,
can be cut loose to float on a room's

air currents, so the phone beside her bed
seems miles away. Miles, too, her need
to answer, though I let it ring and ring,
afraid to imagine, unable to stop her
slipping voiceless into night's hidden limbs.
Dark night, if you are truly sweeter than dawn,

shining at the window, she can see
how she looks, easing out of form, how blurred,
how radiant, in your midnight eye. Now
nothing I say will stop her, and the birds,
wherever they sleep, wings drawn close for warmth,
will wake singing as they always do.

ENDLESS ARGUMENT

A sharp sound in the woods—*whatisit?*
Not a thrush, but a threat crashing the scene,
raucous, like somebody who'd yank the knot

out of a barrel just for the pleasure
of the spill. *Whatisit?* Fast-talking barker,
throat full of static and croak. But stuck here

in the muck, you gotta give it credit
for flapping up and getting where it goes,
making the most out of not much.

Could be a crow. Even in snow
they can hold down a paper plate with one foot
and peel off the congealed cheese. Not bad,

given hard times ahead, a skill, a shill,
a pickpocket saying, *whatisit?*
so you quick look up, and in that split

your wallet's lifted. Bitch if you want,
but somebody's gonna stick around
come winter, somebody's gonna take

all our sweet sad staring off
into infinite vistas, and resist,
insist, *this grit, these guts—this is it.*

COASTAL BOP

At the piano's most plaintive moment a few bars
come and go,   bird quick.   Was it
   really blue, and did it
                          sing, that soul sting, sweet
piercing you want to repeat?

   But now the pace picks up, new themes enter
and break.   To follow you have to run like
   someone on a dock keeping up with the water's
dazzle
                    sun-struck wavelets flashing the sides

   of a boat, shadow
                          and light, little fish
impossible to catch if you haven't done it
   your whole life.   And now it's quickened
                          again, full throttle ahead, open
sea, water rough and frenzied

   like sharks swimming in, everything slashed
                          jagged, splashed—done for
dashed *fractioned fronned dazond*
                                    addun drunned
   structure cut loose, stunned.   Call it
tongues, not chaos, call it casting out

ballast, boat rolling barrels, boxes
                    swept and bunched at the bow,
then bump crash backlash clustered
                    and dumped—sounds we oh so
    quickly insist into words, but
somebody's got to
                    yank them apart

    for us *oost ooze*
                    keep them wild, raw   spray
aaaa in the face, dock swamped, bird
    you never saw *awe* before
                    and ever since what
was that?

ELEGY AND ARGUMENT

Behind the wheel, as my stepdad grew smaller,
he'd stop sometimes halfway into a turn
and wonder where he was going. He'd shake his head
slowly as if to hear some inner GPS,

or as if to wake up and find himself back home
under the twang of wind in metal pie pans
hung from his carport rafters. Pie pans, wind socks,
knotted kite tails—more like some grade school class

had been asked to decorate his retirement complex,
not an old man on a wobbly ladder,
railing at blackbirds. My son says he can't hear it,
but when I shake my head, I can bring back those pans,

their faint aluminum clang, bring back my stepdad's
pursed lips, his soothing sounds, all affection in old age,
deaf to our past debates about fact and feeling,
his endless lectures on goals while I stared at clouds,

drifting inside my head. No surprise
when my daughter wrote in her fourth grade
science report, "The brain looks like a cauliflower,
or a walnut halved." Or when my son shook his head,

as if that kind of thought would send us all back
to the four humours and leeches. He chose
the surgery channel on TV, and my two selves
glared as if each would cancel the other out.

But what fact doesn't come wrapped in feeling?
And surely feelings need facts the way rivers
need banks, not to mention the way bankers
need rivers, and my stepfather needed his boat

to entertain adjusters, appraisers, directors,
men who lived by numbers, but didn't count
on bottom muck and eelgrass oozing into
their sharp talk of expenditure and return.

What spoke louder to me was my stepdad weeping
beside his aged dog, his growing teary
over any gesture of love he didn't have
to bully or earn, his pride in both my children,

so finally we agreed, it's all mingled:
my son who knows ligament, muscle, bone
in English and Latin, my daughter who reads
the subtlest feelings that flicker across a face,

two sides of the brain I long to see embrace,
or shake enough to make that tuning fork hum,
aftermath of plucked strings, small hint of music
feeling its way through substance after substance:

cauliflower, walnut, skull, old man fussing
over blackbirds that mess his car, hanging
more spinning, clattering contraptions,
as if sun splatter and sound haven't already

filled to overflowing those winged tricksters.
"*My car, my car,*" his gestures seemed to insist—
driven by feeling as his skills diminished?
Fact is, long after it hurt him to get in

and out of the car, long after it was safe
to sit beside him, I'd sit beside him
who had nothing to do with my conception,
but who fathered me just the same.

TO THE INFINITESIMAL

I opened a holy book hoping to find
the part about turning the other cheek,
and out you flew, hovering dot

smaller than a comma, winged inkling.
Were you late when names were given out,
an afterthought, spittle from a cough

at the end of creation? Feeling you
graze my cheek, I lunged like a clumsy golem,
but you gave me the slip.

How can anything so small have a will,
a want, the wits to flee two clapped hands?
In a time revving for war, with experts

stoking the engines, insisting necessity,
you're a nil, a naught, a nuisance to ignore,
not one of mystery's vexing ellipses...

If your wings whir, if you buzz at all,
it's below our hearing, little serif
broken off some word in holy writ

to drift among us, inaudible
argument illustrating creation's
fondness for every last tittle and jot.

EVERY NOTE

It's that moment the music stops,
the second before hands lift to applaud,
which we would prolong if we could, slip out
without speaking, to hold that instant
just before chairs scrape and conversations
resume over the parking lot's gravel—

or it's the moment we first step
out of the museum, and the moon's newly
minted, fir trees having shrugged into night's
thick shaggy coat, as stars salt the sky,
and everything's designed, shaped for delight
or swirled in a fevered moment of swoon,

as when we lie in a sweet tangle of limbs,
and it seems the outer atoms of our flesh
have blended, so you move an arm, Love,
but it's not the one you thought was yours,
while I rub your back and almost feel inside
your spine's sinuous assent,

that mystery of a seamless urge, when silence
just after music is filled with every note,
the way light holds an entire spectrum,
or just after love when our separate thoughts
are still only of love: what isn't love,
or music or light, we ask ourselves then.

LIFE AND HOLINESS

I couldn't finish the book because the end
no longer existed, the final words on *life*
and *holiness,* that old coin with its two sides
impossible to see at once, so each face
makes you long for the other—unless, of course,
the coin's been rubbed down, almost out,
as my book was, not dog-*eared,* but dog-*chewed,*
its upper corners gnawed to raggedy pulp,
a big chunk torn off its lower right,
and the whole book ending coverless
on page 118, so it's hard to read
the thoughts without thinking of their fate,
the message bound to what carries it:
Life and Holiness by Thomas Merton,
bound to our dog named Dreug, Russian for *friend,*
who also ate the edge of my purple dress
as I sat talking on the couch, plus a wooden apple,
and every chair rung in the house. It's hard
not to think of the monk being chewed on
by silence, gnawed down, past ritual and custom,
to a desert of naked prayer, a dark night
where nothing's left but the self's empty shell,
the soul cracked open for something else to rush in,
which the words were just getting to
when Dreug, that zealous friend, aching and driven,
turned the matter into slobber and wag,
his new teeth editing, so the book
ends with:
                              ...For such... (crunch)
      ...lovers of God, all things, whether they appear...
          ...in actuality good. All things manifest the...
              ...All things enable them to grow in...

Here it stops, the promise digested,
our big brown dog a better reader than I,
licking his lips, swallowing the words, taking in
the *such* and *all things,* however they appear.
And were they, *in actuality,* good?
Was the back cover, the spine glue, the wood
or rag pulp of each missing page? "Complete
and unabridged," it says just where the teeth marks
bite, where the paper's rough edge, its newly exposed
microscopic threads meet air and morning light,
as if words could turn into life, into window glass
with bickering sparrows, children walking
to school, as Dreug, with his spotted face,
his feathery toes, watches *all things*
manifest the— enable them to grow in—
As to holiness, you lovers of God, must all things
come to an edge where words stop, and hunger—
that faithful friend who eats away what once
would have been so easy to read—begins?

RECENT TITLES FROM Alice James Books

Shelter, Carey Salerno
The Next Country, Idra Novey
Begin Anywhere, Frank Giampietro
The Usable Field, Jane Mead
King Baby, Lia Purpura
The Temple Gate Called Beautiful, David Kirby
Door to a Noisy Room, Peter Waldor
Beloved Idea, Ann Killough
The World in Place of Itself, Bill Rasmovicz
Equivocal, Julie Carr
A Thief of Strings, Donald Revell
Take What You Want, Henrietta Goodman
The Glass Age, Cole Swensen
The Case Against Happiness, Jean-Paul Pecqueur
Ruin, Cynthia Cruz
Forth A Raven, Christina Davis
The Pitch, Tom Thompson
Landscapes I & II, Lesle Lewis
Here, Bullet, Brian Turner
The Far Mosque, Kazim Ali
Gloryland, Anne Marie Macari
Polar, Dobby Gibson
Pennyweight Windows: New & Selected Poems, Donald Revell
Matadora, Sarah Gambito
In the Ghost-House Acquainted, Kevin Goodan
The Devotion Field, Claudia Keelan
Into Perfect Spheres Such Holes Are Pierced, Catherine Barnett
Goest, Cole Swensen
Night of a Thousand Blossoms, Frank X. Gaspar
Mister Goodbye Easter Island, Jon Woodward
The Devil's Garden, Adrian Matejka
The Wind, Master Cherry, the Wind, Larissa Szporluk

Alice James Books has been publishing exclusively poetry since 1973. One of the few presses in the country that is run collectively, the cooperative selects manuscripts for publication through both regional and national annual competitions. New regional authors become active members of the cooperative, participating in the editorial decisions of the press. The press, which historically has placed an emphasis on publishing women poets, was named for Alice James, sister of William and Henry, whose fine journal and gift for writing went unrecognized within her lifetime.

TYPESET AND DESIGNED BY MIKE BURTON

Printed by Thomson-Shore
on 30% postconsumer recycled paper
processed chlorine-free